Leshaan Sena – Leshaan Englesnaaye
English-Senaya Dictionary

Laura McPherson

with Paul Caldani and Allegra Olson

2014

Dedication

For the Chaldean community of Sanandaj,
ta kole soraaye sena, for the future.

Notes on spelling and pronunciation

Senaya is traditionally written in the Syriac alphabet, which is used to write other Aramaic languages like Assyrian or Modern Chaldean. Unlike English, this alphabet is written from right to left, and it is related to the Hebrew and Arabic alphabets. In this chapter, we include a chart of the Syriac script and encourage anyone interested in learning it to check out online resources, such as this tutorial on the alphabet: http://www.learnassyrian.com/aramaic/.
The example words are in Assyrian, but the alphabet and pronunciation remain largely the same.

To make it easier to learn, we have developed an alphabet for Senaya that uses the Roman alphabet. This not only relieves the burden of having to learn a new language and new alphabet simultaneously, but also makes it easier to use Senaya in media like e-mail or text messages. With limitations of the English keyboard in mind, we have avoided the use of unusual letters or diacritics, which are often employed in more standard romanizations of Aramaic dialects. In the chart that follows, we will point out how the sounds are written in our alphabet along with the "standard" or scholarly romanization scheme (used, for example, in Panoussi 1990):

Alphabet	Romanization	Sounds like...
aa	ā	f<u>a</u>ther
a	a	b<u>us</u>
b	b	<u>b</u>us
ch	č	<u>ch</u>eese
d	d	<u>d</u>og
ee	ē	p<u>ay</u>
e	e	p<u>i</u>t
f	f	<u>f</u>ather
g	g	<u>g</u>o
gh	ğ	like French <u>r</u>ouge or Persian otaa<u>q</u>
h	h	<u>h</u>ow
ii	ī	<u>see</u>
j	j	<u>j</u>ar
k	k	<u>c</u>ar
l	l	<u>l</u>ove
l*	ḷ	(a stronger

		version of *l*)
m	m	<u>m</u>o<u>m</u>
m*	ṃ	(a stronger version of *m*)
n	n	<u>n</u>oo<u>n</u>
oo	ō	fl<u>ow</u>
o	o	b<u>oo</u>k
p	p	<u>p</u>ut
q	q	(a throaty version of *k*)
r	r	(like Spanish *r*)
r*	ṛ	(a stronger version of *r*)
s	s	<u>s</u>ing
s*	ṣ	(a stronger version of *s*)
t	t	<u>t</u>ell
t*	ṭ	(a stronger version of *t*)
uu	ū	f<u>oo</u>d
w	w	<u>w</u>ater
x	x	like German Ba<u>ch</u>
y	y	<u>y</u>ellow
z	z	<u>z</u>oo
'	'	uh<u>-</u>oh

Senaya-English Dictionary

&	c	(no English equivalent)

'aahenger *n* blacksmith

'aala *n* God (see also **'alaaha**)

'aana *n* I

'aanii *n* they

'aaraayesh *n* make-up

'aas*ar *n* evening

'aasán *adj* easy

'aasen *n* iron

'aawa *n* he

'aaxa *adv* here

'aayat *n* you (f. sg.)

'aayet *n* you (m. sg.)

'abaaya *n* long robe (for men)

'agran *adj* expensive

'ahmaq *adj* stupid; idiot

'ainek *n* glasses

'al&aan *adv* just now

'alaaha *n* god (see also **'aala**)

'alaaha zadaaya *cpd adj* God-fearing

'albaluu *n* sour cherry

'alpa *num* thousand

'ama *n* paternal uncle

'amriikaaya (pl. amrikaaye) *n, adj* American

'amta *n* aunt paternal aunt

'an *det* these

'andaaza *n* size

'apesqoopa (pl. 'apesqoope) *n* bishop

'aqla (pl. 'aqlaase; 'aqle) *n* foot; leg

'aqobra (pl. 'aqobre) *n* mouse

'aqorwa (pl. 'aqorwaase; 'aqorwe) *n* scorpion

'ara (pl. 'are) *n* floor

'arba *num* four

'arbaasar *num* fourteen

'arbii *num* forty

'arbúshaaba *n* Wednesday

'armoot*a (pl. 'armoot*e) *n* pomegranate

'armoot*ad 'aqla (pl. 'armoot*ed; 'aqlaase) *n* knee

'armoot*ad 'iida *n* elbow

'aruusii *n* stained glass

'arzan *adj* cheap

'as*l *n* origin

'as*ra (pl. 'as*rawaase) *n* town

'asbab baazi *n+n* toy

'ashpaz *n* cook

'ashpesxaana *n* kitchen

'atiiqa (pl. 'atiiqe) *adj* old

'aw ('oo) *det* those (distal)

'aw ('oo) *det* that

'axarsar *adv* eventually

'axnii *n* we

'axoona (pl. 'axonwaase) *n* brother

'axtooxon *n* you (pl.)

'ay ('ey) *det* this

'aziiza (pl. 'aziize) *n* darling; beloved

'e&chaasar *num* nineteen

'ebra (pl. bnoone; 'ebre) *n* boy; son

'edyúu *adv* today

'eeda (pl. 'eedawaase) *n* feast

'eeda r*aaba (pl. 'eedawaase r*aabe) *n+adj* Easter

'eeda zoora (pl. 'eedawaase zoore) *n+adj* Christmas

'eeka *adj* where

'eena (pl. 'eene; 'eenaase) *n* eye

'eena (pl. 'eene) *n* spring; stream

'eena xwarta *n+adj* white of the eye

'eewa (pl. 'eewe) *n* cloud

'ejaara *n* rent

'ekma *wh* how many

'el *prep* on

'em *wh* which

'emtahan *n* test; exam

'englesnaaya (pl. 'englesnaaye) *n, adj* English

'epra (pl. 'epre) *n* dirt

'epra smooqa *n+ adj* clay

'es*ra *num* ten

'es*rii *num* twenty

'eshta *num* six

'eshtaasar *num* sixteen

'eshtii *num* sixty

'etee *v* have

'evengalion *n* Bible

'exre *n* shit

'eza (pl. 'eze) *n* goat

'ezla (pl. 'ezle) *n* thread

'iibee *v.* can

'iida (pl. 'iidaase) *n* hand

'iigarta *n* St. Paul's epistles

'iiliipa (pl. 'iiliipe) *adj* learned; knowledgeable

'iiman *comp* when

'iisho'a *n* Jesus

'iisoqsa (pl. 'iisoqyaase) *n* ring

'iitalyaaya (pl. 'iitalyaaye) *n, adj* Italian

'iixaala *n* food

'iizart*a *n* veiled robe (for women)

'ol *n* promise

'omma *num* hundred

'on *det* those (proxal)

'oome *prep* across from

'oomid *n* hope

'oodidwar *adj* hopeful

'ooya *n* she

'opaache *n* cloth

'orba *n* sheep

'oroota (pl. orotwaase) *n* Friday

'orxa (pl. 'orxe) *n* road

'ostaad *n* professor; maestro

'ot*ma *n* thigh, hip

'otaaq *n* thigh, hip

b

baaba (pl. baabawaase) *n* father

baaba r*aaba (pl. baabawaase r*aabe) *n+adj* grandfather

baaba shmayaana *n+adj* heavenly father

baaqa (pl. baaqe) *n* mosquito

baaxesh *phrase* excuse me (to step out)

badla (pl. badle) *n* cape-like church robe worn around the neck

bahaar *n* spring

bahosh *adj* smart

baloota *n* throat

banayuusa *n* building; construction

banjanta komta (pl. banjaane koome) *n+adj* eggplant

banjanta smoqta (pl. banjaane smooqe) *n+adj* tomato

baraay *n, adj* outside

barzara barzare *n* seeds

bas*r *n* behind

bashlaana *n* cook

basiima (pl. basiime) *adj* sweet

basta (pl. baste) *n* package

bastorma *n* ground meat dish

baxta (pl. 'enshe; 'eshenyaase; baxte) *n* woman; wife

beeriixt *adj* ugly

bees qorwaase *n+n* cemetery

beesa (pl. beesawaase; beese) *n* house

beeta (pl. beete) *n* egg

belxoodee *adv* by oneself

berga *n* nook; cranny; hole

bes*la (pl. bes*le) *n* onion

besh *adv* more

beshtom *adj* better

besma (pl. besme) *n* incense

betelhem *n* nativity

biibar (pl. biibaare) *n* pepper

biibii 'eene *n* pupils

biisha (pl. biishe) *n* sinner

bleel *n* above

bleel 'eena *n+n* eyelid (Lit. above the eye)

bloq *n* blister

boghdaaye *adv* together

bogiin nasyaase *n+n* ear canals

bogiin pooqa *n+n* nostril

bogiina *n* forehead

boqalamon *n* turkey

borka (pl. borkaase) *n* knee

braata (pl. bnaase) *n* girl; daughter

breshyág *adj* shining

briixuusa *n* congratulations; greetings

ch

chaarak *n* quarter

chaay *n* tea

chabaana (pl. chabaane) *n* well; trench

chakma (pl. chakme) *n* boot

chanaaka *n* chin

chap *adj* left

chelme *n* snot

cheshma (pl. chesme) *n* restroom

chinaasha *n* no one

chon *conj* because

d

---

daamán *n* skirt

daftarcha (pl. daftarche) *n* notebook

danwa (pl. danwe) *n* tail

daqiiqa (pl. daqiiqe) *n* minute

dar*maana (pl. dar*maane) *n* medicine

dars *n* studies

darta (pl. dartawaase; darte) *n* yard

dashta (pl. dashtaane dashtawaase) *n* woods; forest; desert

daskeesha (pl. daskeeshe) *n* glove

dax *adv* how

---

dedwa (pl. dedwe) *n* fly (insect)

deeda (pl. deedawaase) *n* breast

deefa (pl. deefe) *n* guest

deewa (pl. deewe) *n* wolf

deewa *n* gold

defiisa (pl. defyaase) *n* party

dema *n* blood

denaana *adj* owing

deqna *n* beard

diika (pl. diike) *n* rooster without a crest

docharxa (pl. docharxe) *n* bicycle

dokaana (pl. dokaane) *n* store

doks qorbaana *n+n* compartment in altar; communion safe

doksa (pl. doksaane) *n* place

doktor (pl. doktore) *n* doctor

doroshka (pl. doroshke) *n* cart

dowrii (pl. dowryaase) *n* plate

drang *adj, adv* late

duniye *n* world

duusha (pl. duushe) *n* honey

dxaalat *n* interference

f

faleena *n* undershirt

faqat *adv* only

farmayshot ('el 'eenii) *phrase* You're
welcome (on my eyes)

farsii *n, adj* Persian; Farsi

fekr *n* thought

fil *n* elephant

fransa *n* France

fransaaya (pl. fransaaye) *adj* French

g

---

gaaloosha (pl. gaalooshe) *n* rubber boots

gaare *n* roof

ganaawa *n* thief

gapiita (pl. gapiite) *n* small chapel

garma (pl. garme) *n* bone

garshuunii *n* version

gaw *prep* in

gaw 'ajala *p+n* quickly

gela (pl. gele) *n* grass

gelda (pl. gelde) *n* skin

gerek *aux* must

---

gexka (pl. gexke) *n* smile

ghdeesar *num* eleven

goldán (pl. goldaane) *n* vase

gomla (pl. gomle) *n* camel

goochaana (pl. goochaane) *n* cane

goora (pl. goore; goorawaase) *n* man; husband

gooza (pl. gooze) *n* walnuts

gopa (pl. gopaape; gope) *n* cheek

gopta *n* cheese

gorwa (pl. gorwe) *n* socks

guuda (guudawaase; guude) *n* wall

gwaara (pl. gwaare) *n* marriage

gyaana *n* body; self

h

---

hawd*a (pl. hawd*e) *n* pond

ham *adv* also

hamam *n* bath

har daf&a *adv* always

haruuqa (pl. haruuqe) *adj* far

hawa (pl. hawe) *adj* fine; good

hawaa *n* weather

hazm *n+v* digest

hemanuusa *n* faith

hiilaana (pl. hiilaane) *n* tree

hkeesa (pl. hkeyaase) *n* story

hobba *n* love

hoshyar *adj* careful

---

huuraara (pl. huuraare) *n* sash (for church robes)

j

---

jaada (pl. jaade) *n* road

jam *n* handful

jama&at *n* community; group

jang *n* war

jaraah*ii *n* surgery

jele *n* clothes

jiger *n* liver

joght *adj* evil

jowanqa (pl. jowanqe; joonaqyaase) (f) *adj, n* young; youth

junúb *n, adv* south

---

juujala (pl. juujale) *n* small game hen; chick

k

---

kaagál *n* mudbrick

kaahuu *n* lettuce

kaaka (pl. kaake) *n* tooth

kaalak *n* melon

kaaluu (pl. kaaluwe) *n* bride; doll

kaasa (pl. kaase) *n* stomach

kaasa w piilaasa *n conj n* chalice and plate (for communion)

kabiira *adv* a lot

kaf 'iida *n+n* palm of the hand

kafiya *n* hankerchief; cloth napkin

kalasher (pl. kalashere) *n* rooster with crest

---

kalba (pl. kalbe) *n* dog

kalepsa (pl. kalepse) *n* bitch

kamas*ra (pl. kamas*re) *n* pear

kara *n* butter

karma (pl. karmaane) *n* field

kbee *v* want

keelee *phrase* where is it?

kerya (pl. kerye) *adj* short

kestakta (pl. kestaade) *n* shoes

klas *n* class

klochta (pl. kluuche; klooche) *n* cookies

kma*n* mouth

koba 'ezla *n+n* ball of yarn

kod *quant* each

kod daf&a (alt. kol daf&a) *adv* always

kol *quant* all

kolfat *n* servant

komaj *n* small room at the top of the stairs before stepping onto the roof

koodan *adj* stupid; slow

kooma (pl. koome) *adj* black

kooreshk (pk. kooreshke) *n* rabbit

koosa *n* hair (on the head)

kordaaya (pl. kordaaye) *n, adj* Kurdish

korkmaana (pl. korkmaane) *adj* yellow

kot *n* coat

koxwa (pl. koxwe) *n* star

kpiina (pl. kpiine) *adj* hungry

krawát *n* tie

kseesa (pl. kseyaase) *n* chicken

ksiisa (pl. ksiyaase) *n* hat

ksuuta (pl. ksuuyaase) *n* book

kuliisa (pl. kuliyaase) *n* kidney

l

---

laala (pl. laalawaase; laale) *n* maternal uncle

laane *n* nest

laqa *v* kick

lastik *n* tire

laxma (pl. laxme) *n* bread

leba (pl. lebawaase) *n* heart

leele (pl. leelawaase) *n* night

leesha (pl. leeshe) *n* dough

leshaana (pl. leshaane) *n* tongue; language

luula (pl. luule) *n* pipe

---

m

m*aaya *n* water

m*aaya qodshe *n + adj* holy water

ma&aaza (pl. ma&aaze) *n* store

má&da (pl. má&de) *n* stomach

maar*an *n* our lord; holiness

maasa (pl. maswaase) *n* village

maashiin (pl. maashiine) *n* car

mabresh *adj* shining

mabyaana *adj* selfish

maasa

mabyata *n* fast (from all food)

madepha (pl. madephe) *n* altar

madrasa (pl. madrase) *n* school

maghréb *n, adv* west

maghruur *adj* proud; selfish

mahkeesa *n* tale; something to say

maleksa (pl. malekyaase) *n* queen

malka (pl. malke) *n* king

maluuxa *adj* salty

man *pro* who

maqa *wh* how much

máqas* (pl. maqaas*e) *n* scissors

mara (pl. mare) *n* pain

marbut *n* connection

maregla (pl. maregle) *n* copper pot for cooking

mariizxaana (pl. mariizxaane) *n* hospital

mashréq *n, adv* east

mat*ra *n* rain

matraan (pl. matraane) *n* bishop

mazra&a (pl. mazra&e) *n* farm; farmfield

medaad (pl. medaade) *n* pencil

mee *wh* what

melxa (pl. melxe) *n* salt

men *prep* from

mendii (pl. mendiyaane) *n* thing

merra (pl. merre) *n* mirror

meshx heewanii *n+n* animal shortening

meshxa (pl. meshxe) *n* oil

mesta (pl. meste) *n* hair

mez (pl. meeze) *n* table

mo&adab *adj* polite

mo&alam (pl. mo&alame) *n* teacher

moch iida *n+n* wrist

mohandes *n* engineer

mohasel *n* student

momkeniilee *aux* might

mooqa *n* time

moosa *n* death

moqra *n* yolk

moxa *adj* like

mshiihaaya (pl. mshiihaaye) *n* Christian

naasaq *adj* unwell

naasha (pl naashe) *n* person

narm *adj* soft

nasyata (pl. nasyaase) *n* ear

nazar *n* meanness; bad feeling

negaraan *n* worry

nezgera *n* hiccup

nok *n* beak

noxraaya (pl. noxraaye) *n* stranger

nuuniisa *n* fish

nuura *n* fire

p

---

paapa *n* pope

paghra *n* flesh; body

páiz *n* autumn

palaasha *n* fighter

palge *n* half

panjera *n* window

paqarta *n* neck

parcha *n* textile

pardeesa *n* paradise

parparoxta (pl. parparoxyaase) *n* butterfly

pas *conj* then

pechpech *n + v* whisper

---

pechyak *n* wrap

pelk *n* eyelash

pelse *n* money

pepeliyaase *n* eyelashes

perd *n* bridge

perma *n* incenser

pes*ra *n* meat

pes*xa *n* Passover

pest*aana *n* dress

piila (pl. piile) *n* elephant

piir *adj* elderly

pip *n* pipe

pl*aasha *n* fight

plekan (pl. plekaane) *n* stair

pooqa *n* nose

pooxa *n* wind

pooxa *n* wind

porpesa *n* in pieces

prezla *n* metal

q

qaala (pl. qaale) *n* voice

qaasha *n* priest

qaashaata (pl. qaashaate) *n* eyebrow

qahwa *n* coffee

qahweya *adj* brown

qala *adj, adv* early; fast

qalaawa *n* crow

qalam basma *cpd n* pencil

qalyán *n* hookah

qam *prep* in front of

qam daawa *adv* before; in the old days

qamaay *adj* first

qameesa *n* past

qamxa *n* flour

qanyaane *n* livestock

qaraane *n* coins

qarchke *n* mushroom

qariila *adj* cold

qarooya *n* lector

qarqara *n* spool of thread

qarsa *adj* cold

qarsa *n* chill

qaryaana *n* reading

qasepkar *n* merchant

qat*uusa (pl. qat*waase) *n* cat

qayaq *n* boat

qdiisha *adj* holy

qeesa *n* log

qeeta *n* summer

qesmat *n* side; part

qiilax *adv* a little

qlop *n* mouthful; gulp

qondaq *n+v* swaddle

qoome *adj* tomorrow

qoora (pl. qoorawaase) *n* grave

qor *prep* next to; near

qorbaana *n* communion wafer

qorqaniisa *n* Adam's apple

qors *n* pills

qorsii *n* table heater

r

---

r*aaba *adj* big

r*aaza *n* mass

r*aza *n* rice

ra&ya *n* farmer; peasant

raanandigii *n* driving

raastii *adj* right

rabaana *n* monk

rabanta *n* nun

raftaar *n* manners

raprapiisa *n* sty

raqaada *n* dancer

reesh mara *n+n* headache

reesha *n* head

---

reewaase *n* wild sour vegetable

reewii *n* fox

renge *n* color

riiya *n* lung

romha *n* spear

roodaana *n* earthquake

rotxaana *n* river

ruuda *n i*ntestine

ruusha (pl. ruushaane) *n* shoulder

s*

s*aabun *n* soap

s*adra *n* chest

s*afar *n* zero

s*alma *n* face

s*aruupa *adj* spicy

s*eera *n* moon

s*epra (pl. s*epre) *n* sparrow

s*es*ra (pl. s*es*re) *n* cockroach, cricket, grasshopper

s*liiwa *n* cross

s*loota (pl. s*lawaase) *n* prayer

s*ooma *n* fasting; Lent

s*orta *n* portrait; face

S

sa&at (pl. sa&ate) *n* watch; hour

saaz *n* making; building

safar *n* trip

san'atgar *n* craftsman

sandalii *n* chair

sapa *n* mouthful; bite

saws *n* sauce

saxt *adj* hard; difficult

seema *n* silver

seepa *n* sword

semlaale *n* mustache

senaaya *adj* Senaya

sendiya *n* watermelon

sepa (pl. sepwaase) *n* lip

setuun (pl. setuune) *n* column

setwa *n* winter

skenta *n* knife

smelta *n* ladder

smooqa (pl. smooqe) *adj* red

sobasta (pl. sobaase) *n* finger

sotaana *n* robe worn by ordained priests

suuraaya (pl. suuraaye) *adj* Christian

suusii (pl. suusii; susyaase) *n* horse

swoya *adj* thirsty

sh

shaagert *n* student

shaapúu *n* round hat with a brim

shaasa *n* fever

shaata (pl. shene; shaate) *n* year

shaayat *adv* maybe

shal *n* shawl

sham'a *n* candle

shamaasha *n* deacon

shansa *n* chance

shanshin *n* dining room; entertaining room

shapiira *adj* beautiful

shapsa *n* Saturday

shapsa *n* week

sharba *n* syrup

shawa *num* seven

shaxiina *adj* hot

shaxnuusa *n* heat

sheede *n* almonds

shekwaniisa (pl. shekwaane) *n* ant

shelmaane *n* Muslims

shelwaale *n* pants

shelya *adj, adv* slow(ly)

shema *n* name

shemsha *n* sun

sheng *n* wild leaf eaten with vinegar

shensa *n* sleep

shensa *n* dream

sher *n* lion

sherma *n* butt; ass

shlaama *n* peace

shlaane *n* apricots

shliiha *n* disciple

shloq *adj* busy

shmaya *n* heaven; sky

shoii *num* seventy

shomál *n, adv* north

shoola *n* work

shoqta *n* shirt

shorsa *n* navel

shwaawe *n* neighbors

shwiisa (pl. shwiyaase) *n* bed

shxoore *n* charcoal

t*

t*aama *adv* there

t*aasii *prep + prop* to me

t*axsa *n* liturgy

t*la'úshaaba *n* Tuesday

t*laa (t*laasa) *num* three

t*laii *num* thirty

t*liiba *n* fiancé

t*ltaasar *num* thirteen

t*ooba *n* punishment

t*op *n* ball

t*rosta *adj* true

t*uura (pl. t*uuraane) *n* mountain

t*uusa *n* example

Senaya-English Dictionary

ta *prep* for

taaza *adj* fresh

tagarg *n* hail

taj *n* crest (rooster)

takaan *n* shock; shake

takaan *n+v* shake

talga *n* snow

talma *n* pot

talmiida *n* student; disciple

tamaata *n* tomato

tamee *adv* why

tanorta *n* clay oven

tara *n* door

tarpa *n* leaf

tawarta (pl. tawaryaase) *n* cow

tejaarat *n+v* trade

temal *adv* yesterday

tesh'ii *num* ninety

tesh&a *num* nine

tiine *n* urine

tmaneesar *num* eighteen

tmanii *num* eighty

tmenya *num* eight

tnaana *n* smoke

tont tont *adv* quickly

toola (pl. toole) *n* worm

toora (pl. tawaryaase) *n* bull

tórshaaba *n* Monday

tree *num* two

treesar *num* twelve

troones *n* table altar for communion

tuuma *n* garlic

W

---

warda (pl. warde)*n* flower

waxt (pl. waxte) *n* time

X

xa *num* one

xa reeza *adv* a little bit

xaala *n* vinegar

xaasa (pl. xaswaase) *n* sister

xabra (pl. xabraane) *n* word

xabuusha *n* apple

xahesh *phrase* please

xajaalat *n+v* be shy

xakma *adj* some

xalta *n* maternal aunt

xalwa *n* yogurt

xamcha *adj* some

xamoosa *adj* sour

xamra *n* wine

xamsha *num* five

xamshaasar *num* fifteen

xamshii *num* fifty

xamshúshaaba *n* Thursday

xar daawa *adv* after that

xate *n* wheat

xayatii *n* tailoring

xelya *adj* beautiful

xelya *n* milk

xema *adj* hot; warm

xena *adj* another

xerta *adj* next; another

xes *prep* under

xes *n* butt

xés shelwaale *n* underwear

xeshka *n* darkness

xesna *n* groom

xiima *adj* sick

xiyaare *n* cucumber

xliiwa *adj* bad

xmaara *n* donkey

xmaata *n* injection

xoday *pro* each other

xolmaane *n* dreams

xoora (pl. xoorawaase) *n* friend

xoosh *n, adj* pleasure; good

xóshaaba *n* Sunday

xoshka *n* morning

xruuwa *adj* bad

xt*iisa *n* guilt

xuwe *n* snake

xwaara *adj* white

xwaruusa *n* egg white

xzuura *n* pig

y

ya&nii *phrase* it means

yaala (pl. yaale) *n* child

yaama *n* ocean

yalda *n* birth

yariixa *adj* long

yarxa (pl. yarxe; yarxaase) *n* month

yawash *adv* slowly

yax *n* ice

yema (pl. yeme) *n* mother

yema r*apsa *n+adj* grandmother

yolpaana *n* knowledge

yooma (pl. yoome) *n* day

yoona (pl. yoone) *n* pigeon

Z

zaaga *n* bell

zaaya *adj* spoiled; rotten

zabnaana *n* seller

zamaara *n* singer

zard*awaala *n* bee

zareng *adj* clever

zeetún *n* olive

zelzela *n* earthquake

zmarta *n* song

zonaare *n* belt (for church robes)

zoora *adj* small

English-Senaya Dictionary

a little *Adv* qiilax

a little bit *Adv* xa reeza

a lot *Adv* kabiira

above *N* bleel

across from *Adv* oomel

Adam's apple *N* qorqaniisa

after that *Adv* xar daawa

all *Quant* kol

almonds *N* sheede

also *Adv* ham

altar *N* madepha (pl. madephe)

altar (for communion) *N* troones

always *Adv* kod daf&a ~ kol daf&a

always *Adv* har daf&a

American *N, Adj* 'amriikaaya (pl. amrikaaye)

another *Adj* xena

another *Adj* xerta

ant *N* shekwaniisa (pl. shekwaane)

apple *N* xabuusha

apricots *N* shlaane

aunt (father's sister) *N* 'amta

aunt (mother's sister) *N* xalta

autumn *N* páiz

b

bad *Adj* xruuwa

bad *Adj* xliiwa

ball *N* t*op

ball of yarn *N+N* koba 'ezla

bath *N* hamam

beak *N* nok

beard *N* deqna

beautiful *Adj* xelya

beautiful *Adj* shapiira

because *conjunction* chon

bed *N* shwiisa (pl. shwiyaase)

bee *N* zard*awaala

before *Adv* qam daawa

behind *N* bas*r

bell *N* zaaga

belt (for church robes) *N* zonaare

better *Adj* beshtom

Bible *N* 'evengalion

bicycle *N* docharxa (pl. docharxe)

big *Adj* r*aaba

birth *N* yalda

bishop *N* 'apesqoopa (pl. 'apesqoope)

bishop *N* matraan (pl. matraane)

bitch *N* kalepsa (pl. kalepse)

bite *N* sapa

black *Adj* kooma (pl. koome)

blacksmith *N* 'aahenger

blister *N* bloq

blood *N* dema

boat *N* qayaq

body *N* paghra

body, self *N* gyaana

bone *N* garma (pl. garme)

book *N* ksuuta (pl. ksuuyaase)

boot *N* chakma (pl. chakme)

boy *N* 'ebra (pl. bnoone, 'ebre)

bread *N* laxma (pl. laxme)

breast *N* deeda (pl. deedawaase)

bride, doll *N* kaaluu (pl. kaaluwe)

bridge *N* perd

brother *N* 'axoona (pl. 'axonwaase)

brown *Adj* qahweya

building *N* banayuusa

building *N* saaz

bull *N* toora (pl. tawaryaase)

busy *Adj* shloq

butt *N* xes

butt *N* sherma

butter *N* kara

butterfly *N* parparoxta (pl.

parparoxyaase)

by oneself *Adv* belxoodee

camel *N* gomla (pl. gomle)

can *V* iibee

candle *N* sham'a

cane *N* goochaana (pl. goochaane)

car *N* maashiin (pl. maashiine)

careful *Adj* hoshyar

cart *N* doroshka (pl. doroshke)

cat *N* qat*uusa (pl. qat*waase)

cemetery *N+N* bees qorwaase

chair *N* sandalii

chalice and plate (for communion) *N conj N* kaasa w piilaasa

chance *N* shansa

chapel (small) *N* gapiita (pl. gapiite)

charcoal *N* shxoore

cheap *Adj* 'arzan

cheek *N* gopa (pl. gopaape, gope)

cheese *N* gopta

chest *N* s*adra

chick *N* juujala (pl. juujale)

chicken *N* kseesa (pl. kseyaase)

child *N* yaala (pl. yaale)

chill *N* qarsa

chin *N* chanaaka

Christian *Adj* suuraaya (pl. suuraaye)

Christian *N* mshiihaaya (pl.
    mshiihaaye)

Christmas *N+Adj* 'eeda zoora (pl. 'eedawaase zoore)

class *N* klas

clay *N+Adj* 'epra smooqa

clever *Adj* zareng

cloth *N* opaache

clothes *N* jele

cloud *N* 'eewa (pl. 'eewe)

coat *N* kot

cockroach *N* s*es*ra (pl. s*es*re)

coffee *N* qahwa

coins *N* qaraane

cold *Adj* qariila

cold *Adj* qarsa

color *N* renge

column *N* setuun (pl. setuune)

communion wafer *N* qorbaana

community *N* jama&at

compartment in altar *N+N* doks
    qorbaana

congratulations *N* briixuusa

connection *N* marbut

construction *N* banayuusa

cook *N* 'ashpaz

cook *N* bashlaana

cookies *N* klochta (pl. kluuche,
    klooche)

cow tawarta (pl. tawaryaase)

craftsman *N* san'atgar

crest (rooster) *N* taj

cricket *N* s*es*ra (pl. s*es*re)

cross *N* s*liiwa

crow *N* qalaawa

cucumber *N* xiyaare

d

---

dancer *N* raqaada

darkness *N* xeshka

darling *N* 'aziiza (pl. 'aziize)

daughter *N* braata (pl. bnaase)

day *N* yooma (pl. yoome)

deacon *N* shamaasha

death *N* moosa

desert *N* dashta (pl. dashtaane, dashtawaase)

difficult *Adj* saxt

digest *N+V* hazm h-w-d

dining room *N* shanshin

dirt *N* 'epra (pl. 'epre)

---

disciple *N* shliiha

disciple *N* talmiida

doctor *N* doktor (pl. doktore)

dog *N* kalba (pl. kalbe)

donkey *N* xmaara

door *N* tara

dough *N* leesha (pl. leeshe)

dream *N* shensa

dreams *N* xolmaane

dress *N* pest*aana

driving *N* raanandigii

e

each *Quant* kod

each other *Pro* xoday

ear *N* nasyata (pl. nasyaase)

ear canals *N+N* bogiin nasyaase

early *Adj* qala

earthquake *N* roodaana

earthquake *N* zelzela

east *N, Adv* mashréq

Easter *N+Adj* 'eeda r*aaba (pl.
'eedawaase r*aabe)

easy *Adj* 'aasán

egg *N* beeta (pl. beete)

egg white *N* xwaruusa

eggplant *N+Adj* banjanta komta (pl. banjaane koome)

eight *Num* tmenya

eighteen *Num* tmaneesar

eighty *Num* tmanii

elbow *N* 'armoot*ad 'iida

elderly *Adj* piir

elephant *N* fil

elephant *N* piila (pl. piile)

eleven *Num* ghdeesar

engineer *N* mohandes

English *N, Adj* 'englesnaaya (pl. 'englesnaaye)

epistles (of St. Paul) *N* 'iigarta

evening *N* 'aas*ar

eventually *Adv* 'axarsár

evil *Adj* joght

example *N* t*uusa

excuse me (to step out) *Phrase*
   baaxesh

expensive *Adj* 'agran

eye *N* 'eena (pl. 'eene, 'eenaase)

eyebrows *N* qaashaata (pl. qaashaate)

eyelash *N* pelk

eyelashes *N* pepeliyaase

eyelid (Lit. above the eye) *N+N*
   bleel 'eena

f

face *N* s*alma

face *N* s*orta

faith *N* hemanuusa

far *Adj* haruuqa (pl. haruuqe)

farm *N* mazra&a (pl. mazra&e)

farmer *N* ra&ya

fast *Adv* qala

fast (from all food) *N* mabyata

fasting *N* s*ooma

father *N* baaba (pl. baabawaase)

feast *N* 'eeda (pl. 'eedawaase)

fever *N* shaasa

fiancé *N* t*liiba

field *N* karma karmaane

fifteen *Num* xamshaasar

fifty *Num* xamshii

fight *N* pl*aasha

fighter *N* palaasha

fine *Adj* hawa (pl. hawe)

finger *N* sobasta (pl. sobaase)

fire *N* nuura

first *Adj* qamaaya

fish *N* nuuniisa

five *Num* xamsha

flesh *N* paghra

floor *N* 'ara 'are

flour *N* qamxa

flower *N* warda (pl. warde)

fly (insect) *N* dedwa (pl. dedwe)

food *N* 'iixaala

foot *N* 'aqla (pl. 'aqlaase, 'aqle)

for *Prep* ta

forehead *N* bogiina

forest *N* dashta (pl. dashtaane,
dashtawaase)

forty *Num* 'arbii

four *Num* 'arba

fourteen *Num* 'arbaasar

fox *N* reewii

France *N* fransa

French *Adj* fransaaya (pl. fransaaye)

fresh *Adj* taaza

Friday *N* 'oroota (pl. orotwaase)

friend *N* xoora (pl. xoorawaase)

from *Prep* men

front (in front of) *Prep* qam

game hen (small) *N* juujala (pl.
juujale)

garlic *N* tuuma

girl *N* braata (pl. bnaase)

glasses *N* &ainek

glove *N* daskeesha (pl. daskeeshe)

goat *N* 'eza (pl. 'eze)

god *N* 'alaaha

God *N* 'aala

God-fearing *Cpd Adj* 'alaaha zadaaya

gold *N* deewa

good *Adj* hawa, xoosh

grandfather *N+Adj* baaba r*aaba (pl.
baabawaase r*aabe)

grandmother *N+Adj* yema r*apsa

grass *N* gela (pl. gele)

grasshopper *N* s*es*ra (pl. s*es*re)

grave *N* qoora (pl. qoorawaase)

greetings *N* briixuusa

groom *N* xesna

ground meat dish *N* bastorma

group *N* jama&at

guest *N* deefa (pl. deefe)

guilt *N* xt*iisa

gulp *N* qlop

h

hail *N* tagarg

hair *N* mesta (pl. meste)

hair (on the head) *N* koosa

half *N* palge

hand *N* 'iida (pl. 'iidaase)

handful *N* jam

hankerchief *N* kafiya

hard *Adj* saxt

hat *N* ksiisa (pl. ksiyaase)

hat (round with a brim) *N* shaapúu

have *V* 'etee

he *N* 'aawa

head *N* reesha

headache *N+N* reesh mara

heart *N* leba (pl. lebawaase)

heat *N* shaxnuusa

heaven *N* shmaya

heavenly father *N+Adj* baaba
   shmayaana

here *Adv* 'aaxa

hiccup *N* nezgera

hip *N* ot*ma

hole *N* berga

holy *Adj* qdiisha

holy water *N+Adj* m*aaya qodshe

honey *N* duusha (pl. duushe)

hookah *N* qalyán

hope *N* oomid

hopeful *N* oomidwar

horse *N* suusii (pl. suusii, susyaase)

hospital *N* mariizxaana (pl. mariizxaane)

hot *Adj* shaxiina

hot *Adj* xema

hour *N* sa&at (pl. sa&ate)

house *N* beesa (pl. beesawaase, beese)

how *Adv* dax

how many *Wh* 'ekma

how much *Wh* maqa

hundred *Num* 'omma

hungry *Adj* kpiina (pl. kpiine)

husband *N* goora (pl. gore, goorawaase)

i

I *N* 'aana

ice *N* yax

in *Prep* gaw

in pieces *Adj* porpesa

incense *N* besma (pl. besme)

incenser *N* perma

injection *N* xmaata

interference *N* dxaalat

intestine *N* ruuda

iron *N* 'aasen

it means *Phrase* y&anii

Italian *N, Adj* 'iitalyaaya (pl. 'iitalyaaye)

j

Jesus *N* 'iisho'a

just now *Adv* 'al&aan

k

kick *N+V* laqa m-x-y

kidney *N* kuliisa (pl. kuliyaase)

king *N* malka (pl. malke)

kitchen *N* 'ashpesxaana

knee *N* borka (pl. borkaase)

knee *N* 'armoot*ad 'aqla (pl. 'armoot*ed 'aqlaase)

knife *N* skenta

knowledge *N* yolpaana

knowledgeable *Adj* 'iiliipa (pl. 'iiliipe)

Kurdish *N, Adj* kordaaya (pl. kordaaye)

ladder *N* smelta

language *N* leshaana (pl. leshaane)

late *Adj, Adv* drang

leaf *N* tarpa

lector *N* qarooya

left *Adj* chap

leg *N* 'aqla (pl. 'aqlaase, 'aqle)

Lent *N* s*ooma

lettuce *N* kaahuu

like *Adj* moxa

lion *N* sher

lip *N* sepa (pl. sepwaase)

liturgy *N* t*axsa

liver *N* jiger

livestock *N* qanyaane

log *N* qeesa

long *Adj* yariixa

love *N* hobba

lung *N* riiya

maestro *N* 'ostaad

make-up *N* 'aaraayesh

making *N* saaz

man *N* goora (pl. goore, goorawaase)

manners *N* raftaar

marriage *N* gwaara (pl. gwaare)

mass *N* r*aaza

maybe *Adv* shaayat

meanness *N* nazar

meat *N* pes*ra

medicine *N* dar*maana (pl. dar*maane)

melon *N* kaalak

merchant *N* qasepkar

metal *N* prezla

might *Aux* momkeniilee

milk *N* xelya

minute *N* daqiiqa (pl. daqiiqe)

mirror *N* merra (pl. merre)

Monday *N* tórshaaba

money *N* pelse

monk *N* rabaana

month *N* yarxa (pl. yarxe, yarxaase)

moon *N* s*eera

more *Adv* besh

morning *N* xoshka

mosquito *N* baaqa (pl. baaqe)

mother *N* yema (pl. yeme)

mountain *N* t*uura (pl. t*uuraane)

mouse *N* 'aqobra (pl. 'aqobre)

mouth *N* kma

mouthful *N* qlop, sapa

mudbrick *N* kaagál

mushroom *N* qarchke

Muslims *N* shelmaane

must *Aux* gerek

mustache *N* semlaale

n

name *N* shema

napkin (cloth) *N* kafiya

nativity *N* betelhem

navel *N* shorsa

near *Prep* qor

neck *N* paqarta

neighbors *N* shwaawe

nest *N* laane

next *Adj* xerta

next to *Prep* qor

night *N* leele (pl. leelawaase)

nine *Num* tesh&a

nineteen *Num* 'e&chaasar

ninety *Num* tesh'ii

no one *N* chinaasha

nook *N* berga

north *N, Adv* shomál

nose *N* pooqa

nostril *N+N* bogiin pooqa

notebook *N* daftarcha (pl. daftarche)

nun *N* rabanta

O

ocean *N* yaama

oil *N* meshxa (pl. meshxe)

old *Adj* 'atiiqa (pl. 'atiiqe)

olive *N* zeetún

on *Prep* 'el

one *Num* xa

onion *N* bes*la (pl. bes*le)

only *Adv* faqat

origin *N* 'as*l

our lord *N* maar*an

outside *N, Adv* baraay

oven (clay) *N* tanorta

owing *Adj* denaana

package *N* basta (pl. baste)

pain *N* mara (pl. mare)

palm of the hand *N+N* kaf 'iida

pants *N* shelwaale

paradise *N* pardeesa

party *N* defiisa (pl. defyaase)

Passover *N* pes*xa

past *N* qameesa

peace *N* shlaama

pear *N* kamas*ra (pl. kamas*re)

peasant *N* ra&ya

pencil *N* medaad (pl. medaade)

pencil *Cpd N* qalam basma

pepper *N* biibar (pl. biibaare)

Persian *N, Adj* farsii

person *N* naasha (pl. naashe)

pig *N* xzuura

pigeon *N* yoona (pl. yoone)

pills *N* qors

pipe *N* pip

pipe *N* luula (pl. luule)

place *N* doksa (pl. doksaane)

plate *N* dowrii (pl. dowryaase)

please *Phrase* xahesh h-w-d

pleasure *N* xoosh

polite *Adj* mo&adab

pomegranate *N* 'armoot*a (pl. 'armoot*e)

pond *N* h*awd*a (pl. h*awd*e)

pope *N* paapa

portrait *N* s*orta

pot *N* talma

pot (copper, for cooking) *N*
maregla (pl. maregle)

prayer *N* s*loota (pl. s*lawaase)

priest *N* qaasha

professor *N* 'ostaad

promise *N* 'ol

proud *Adj* maghruur

punishment *N* t*ooba

pupils *N* biibii 'eene

q

quarter *N* chaarak

queen *N* maleksa (pl. malekyaase)

quickly *P+N, Adv* gaw 'ajala, tont tont

rabbit *N* kooreshk (pl. kooreshke)

rain *N* mat*ra

reading *N* qaryaana

red *Adj* smooqa (pl. smooqe)

rent *N* 'ejaara

restroom *N* cheshma (pl. chesme)

rhubarb *N* reewaase

rice *N* r*aza

right *Adj* raastii

ring *N* 'iisoqsa (pl. 'iisoqyaase)

river *N* rotxaana

road *N* 'orxa (pl. 'orxe)

road *N* jaada (pl. jaade)

robe (cape-like, worn around the neck for church) *N* badla (pl. badle)

robe (long, for men) *N* 'abaaya

robe (veiled, for women) *N* 'iizart*a

robe (worn by ordained priests) *N* sotaana

roof *N* gaare

room *N* otaaq

room (at the top of the stairs before stepping onto the roof) *N* komaj

rooster (with crest) *N* kalasher kalashere

rooster (without a crest) *N* diika (pl. diike)

rotten *Adj* zaaya

rubber boots *N* gaaloosha (pl. gaalooshe)

S

salt *N* melxa (pl. melxe)

salty *Adj* maluuxa

sash (for church robes) *N* huuraara

    (pl. huuraare)

Saturday *N* shapsa

sauce *N* saws

school *N* madrasa (pl. madrase)

scissors *N* máqas* (pl. maqaas*e)

scorpion *N* 'aqorwa (pl. 'aqorwaase,

    'aqorwe)

seeds *N* barzara (pl. barzare)

selfish *Adj* maghruur

selfish` *Adj.* mabyaana

seller *N* zabnaana

Senaya *Adj* senaaya

servant *N* kolfat

seven *Num* shawa

seventy *Num* shoii

shake *N+V* takaan h-w-d

shake *N* takaan

shawl *N* shal

she *N* 'ooya

sheep *N* 'orba

shining *Adj* mabresh

shining *Adj* breshyág

shirt *N* shoqta

shit *N* 'exre

shock *N* takaan

shoes *N* kestakta (pl. kestaade)

short *Adj* kerya kerye

shortening (animal fat) *N+N* meshx

heewanii

shoulder *N* ruusha (pl. ruushaane)

shy (be shy) *N+V* xajaalat g-r-sh

sick *Adj* xiima

side, part *N* qesmat

silver *N* seema

singer *N* zamaara

sinner *N* biisha (pl. biishe)

sister *N* xaasa (pl. xaswaase)

six *Num* 'eshta

sixteen *Num* 'eshtaasar

sixty *Num* 'eshtii

size *N* 'andaaza

skin *N* gelda (pl. gelde)

skirt *N* daamán

sky *N* shmaya

sleep *N* shensa

slow(ly) *Adj, Adv* shelya

slowly *Adv* yawash

small *Adj* zoora

smart *Adj* bahosh

smile *N* gexka (pl. gexke)

smoke *N* tnaana

snake *N* xuwe

snot *N* chelme

snow *N* talga

soap *N* s*aabun

socks *N* gorwa (pl. gorwe)

soft *Adj* narm

some *Adj* xakma

some *Adj* xamcha

son *N* 'ebra (pl. bnoone, 'ebre)

song *N* zmarta

sour *Adj* xamoosa

sour cherry *N* 'albaluu

south *N, Adv* junúb

sparrow *N* s*epra (pl. s*epre)

spear *N* romha

spicy *Adj* s*aruupa

spoiled *Adj* zaaya

spool of thread *N* qarqara

spring *N* 'eena 'eene

spring *N* bahaar

stained glass *N* 'aruusii

stair *N* plekan (pl. plekaane)

star *N* koxwa (pl. koxwe)

stomach *N* kaasa (pl. kaase)

stomach *N* má&da (pl. má&de)

store *N* ma&aaza (pl. ma&aaze)

store *N* dokaana (pl. dokaane)

story *N* hkeesa (pl. hkeyaase)

stranger *N* noxraaya (pl. noxraaye)

stream *N* 'eena (pl. 'eene)

student *N* mohasel, shaagert, talmiida

studies *N* dars

stupid *Adj* koodan, 'ahmaq

sty *N* raprapiisa

summer *N* qeeta

sun *N* shemsha

Sunday *N* xóshaaba

surgery *N* jaraah*ii

swaddle *N+V* qondaq h-w-d

sweet *Adj* basiima (pl. basiime)

sword *N* seepa

syrup *N* sharba

table *N* mez (pl. meeze)

table heater *N* qorsii

tail *N* danwa (pl. danwe)

tailoring *N* xayatii

tale *N* mahkeesa

tea *N* chaay

teacher *N* mo&alam (pl. mo&alame)

ten *Num* 'es*ra

test, exam *N* 'emtahán

textile *N* parcha

that *Det* 'aw ('oo)

then *Conj* pas

there *Adv* t*aama

these *Det* 'an

they 'aanii

thief *N* ganaawa

thigh *N* ot*ma

thing *N* mendii (pl. mendiyaane)

thirsty *Adj* swoya

thirteen *Num* t*ltaasar

thirty *Num* t*laii

this *Det* 'ay ('ey)

those (distal) *Det* 'aw ('oo)

those (proxal) *Det* 'on

thought *N* fekr

thousand *Num* 'alpa

thread *N* 'ezla (pl. 'ezle)

three *Num* t*laa ~ t*laasa

throat *N* baloota

Thursday *N* xamshúshaaba

tie *N* krawát

time *N* mooqa

time *N* waxt (pl. waxte)

tire *N* lastik

to me *Prep+Pro* t*aasii

today *Adv* 'edyúu

together *Adv* boghdaaye

tomato *N* tamaata

tomato *N+Adj* banjanta smoqta (pl. banjaane smooqe)

tomorrow *Adj* qoome

tongue *N* leshaana (pl. leshaane)

tooth *N* kaaka (pl. kaake)

town *N* 'as*ra (pl. 'as*rawaase)

toy *N+N* 'asbab baazi

trade *N+V* tejaarat h-w-d

tree *N* hiilaana (pl. hiilaane)

trench *N* chabaana (pl. chabaane)

trip *N* safar

true *Adj* t*rosta

Tuesday *N* t*la'úshaaba

turkey *N* boqalamon

twelve *Num* treesar

twenty *Num* 'es*rii

two *Num* tree

ugly *Adj* beeriixt

uncle (father's brother) *N* 'ama

uncle (mother's brother) *N* laala

(pl. laalawaase, laale)

under *Prep* xes

undershirt *N* faleena

underwear *N* xés shelwaale

unwell *Adj* naasaq

urine *N* tiine

V

vase *N* goldán (pl. goldaane)

version *N* garshuunii

village *N* maasa (pl. maswaase)

vinegar *N* xaala

voice *N* qaala (pl. qaale)

wall *N* guuda (pl. guudawaas, guude)

walnuts *N* gooza (pl. gooze)

want *V* kbee

war *N* jang

warm *Adj* xema

watch *N* sa&at (pl. sa&ate)

water *N* m*aaya

watermelon *N* sendiya

we *N* 'axnii

weather *N* hawaa

Wednesday *N* 'arbúshaaba

week *N* shapsa

well *N* chabaana (pl. chabaane)

west *N, Adv* maghréb

what *Wh* mee

wheat *N* xate

when *Comp* 'iiman

where *Adv* 'eeka

where is it? *phrase* keelee

which *Wh* 'em

whisper *N+V* pechpech h-k-y

white *Adj* xwaara

white of the eye *N+Adj* 'eena xwarta

who *Pro* man

why *Adv* tamee

wife *N* baxta (pl. enshe, 'eshenyaase,

　　baxte)

wild leaf (eaten with vinegar) *N*

　　sheng

wind *N* pooxa

window *N* panjera

wine *N* xamra

winter *N* setwa

wolf *N* deewa (pl. deewe)

woman *N* baxta (pl. 'enshe,
   'eshenyaase, baxte)

woods *N* dashta (pl. dashtaane,
   dashtawaase)

word *N* xabra (pl. xabraane)

work *N* shoola

world *N* duniye

worm *N* toola (pl. toole)

worry *N* negaraan

wrap *N* pechyak

wrist *N+N* moch iida

Y

yard *N* darta (pl. dartawaase, darte)

year *N* shaata (pl. shene, shaate)

yellow *Adj* korkmaana (pl. korkmaane)

yesterday *Adv* temal

yogurt *N* xalwa

yolk *N* moqra

you (f. sg.) *N* 'aayat

you (m. sg.) *N* 'aayet

you (pl.) *N* 'axtooxon

You're welcome (on my eyes)

    Phrase farmayshot ('el 'eenii)

young *Adj* jowanqa (m.pl. jowanqe, f.pl.

    joonaqyaase)

youth *N* jowanqa (m.pl. jowanqe, f.pl.

joonaqyaase)

Z

---

zero *N* s*afar

List of verb roots

'-m-r	say
'-s-y	come
'-sh-q	love
'-z-l	go
b-n-y	build
b-q-r	beg, ask
b-r-k	kneel
b-s-m	be healthy
b-sh-l	cook
b-x-sh	forgive
b-x-y	cry
ch-h-y	be tired
d-'-r	come back
d-'-s	sweat
d-&-sh	step on, run over
d-m-x	sleep
d-r-s	vomit
d-r-y	put
d-y-f	invite

d-y-q	play (percussion)
f-r-j	look at, watch
g-d-l	knit
g-n-w	seize, steal
g-r-sh	draw, paint
g-r-y	shave
g-w-r	marry
g-x-k	laugh, smile
gh-d-r	turn around
h-k-y	speak
h-n-q	choke, drown
h-w-d	do
h-w-y	be, become
h-y-k	scratch
h-y-w	give
j-m-&	get together, meet
j-w-b	answer
j-y-l	look in
k-m-y	be named
k-p-n	be hungry
k-s-w	write
k-sh-f	demolish
k-w-sh	come down, jump

k-y-m	become black
l-'-s	lick, chew
l-p-l	fall
&-l-q	be stuck
l-w-sh	wear
m-&-l	scream
m-&-l-q	hang up
m-b-y	be selfish
m-k-?-p	bow (head)
m-k-r-m	make yellow
m-k-r-y	make short
m-k-y-m	dye black
m-l-y	be crowded
m-n-sh-y	forget
m-n-t*-y	take with
m-p-sh	put on clothes (tr)
m-q-d-sh	bless
m-q-l-w	clean
m-q-s	lose weight
m-r-y	hurt
m-r-y-sh	wake (sb) up
m-s-k-r	lose

m-s-m-q	make red
m-s-w-y	fix, repair
m-s-y	scrub (clothes)
m-s*-l-y	pray for, bless
m-sh-h	oil
m-sh-t-x	find
m-sh-y	scrub (car, floor, table), erase
m-t*-	get wet
m-t*-r	keep
m-t*-y	reach
m-x-w-r	make white
m-x-w-y	pretend, appear, show?
m-x-y	hit, beat, paste
m-y-l-p	teach
m-y-q-d	burn
m-y-q-r	respect
m-y-r-q	grow (tr)
m-y-r-x	make long
m-y-s	die
m-z-y-d	gain weight
n-&-s	bite
n-p-x	be swollen

n-q-z	wink
n-sh-q	kiss
n-t*-r	keep, take care of
n-w-x	bark
n-x-p	be shy
n-x-r	slaughter
p-l-l	distribute
p-l-q	leave, exit
p-l-t*	pull out
p-l*-sh	fight
p-q-y	explode, crack
p-r-sh	separate
p-r-x	fly
p-s-y	walk
p-sh-q	translate
p-sh-r	melt
p-y-sh	remain, stay
q-l-y	fry
q-r-y	read, study
q-s*-y	cut
q-t*-l	kill
q-t*-y	cut

q-y-m	get up
r-k-w	ride
r-p-s	blink
r-q-d	dance
r-x-t*	run
&-r-y	hold
r-y-sh	wake up
s-k-r	be drunk
s-m-q	become red, blush
s-m-x	stop, stand, wait
s-p-k	become empty
s-p-r	be patient
s-q-l	decorate
s-r-x	call
s-w-y	get better, make
s-x-y	swim
s*-l-y	pray
sh-'-l	cough
sh-d-r	send
sh-l-x	take off
sh-m-y	hear, listen
sh-p-x	pour, scatter
sh-q-l	buy, obtain

sh-r-y	start
sh-t-y	drink
sh-w-q	leave behind
t-'-l	play
t-l-q	throw away
t-w-r	break
t-w-y	cost
t-x-r	remember
t*-l-b	propose
t*-sh-y	hide
'-x-l	eat
x-l-l	wash with water
x-l-m	be fat
x-l-s*	finish
x-t-y	sew
x-w-r	become white
x-w-t*	mix
x-z-y	see
y-l-d	give birth
y-l-p	learn
y-q-d	be burned
y-q-r	be respected

y-r-q	grow (intr)
y-s-q	climb
y-t-w	sit
y-w-r	enter
y-w-sh	be dry
z-b-n	sell
z-l-m	hurt, injure
z-m-r	sing
z-ng-r	echo
z-r-y	plant

Senaya-English Dictionary

Senaya-English Dictionary